Walking Where God Walks

Carol Bo Howell

Walking Where God Walks. Copyright 2019 Carol Bo Howell. Produced and printed by Stillwater River Publications. All rights reserved. Written and produced in the United States of America. This book may not be reproduced or sold in any form without the expressed, written permission of the author and publisher.

Visit our website at www.StillwaterPress.com for more information.

First Stillwater River Publications Edition

Library of Congress Control Number: 2019908210

ISBN-13: 978-1-950339-18-1
ISBN-10: 1-950339-18-1

12345678910
Written by Carol Bo Howell
Published by Stillwater River Publications, Pawtucket, RI 02860

(All Scriptures are quoted from the King James Bible, except for Romans 8:9 and John 14:15, as noted).

The views and opinions expressed in this book ae solely those of the author and do not necessarily reflect the views and opinions of the publisher.

Dedication

This little book of miracles is dedicated to
The God of all Creation, Jehovah,
Who Is The Creator of all that is Good
and of all that is Beautiful.

This includes the discovery of adventure
and of personal revelation.

Endorsement

"Every God-loving woman should read this book, be revived in her destiny, and understand the possibilities of her own personal walk with God."

> ~Sid Roth
> Messianic Vision / It's Supernatural
> 4301 Westinghouse Boulevard
> Charlotte, North Carolina 28273

Taken from John 5:19 and 30; 8:26; and 14:10 KJV

"I do nothing but what

I see the Father doing.

And I say nothing but what

I hear the Father saying."

Table of Contents

To the Reader 7

Why Are You About to Read This Little Book? 8

We May All Be Asking the Same Question! 12

Chapter 1 – God Moved in The Established Church 17

Chapter 2 – Your Gifts and Your Callings from God 21

Chapter 3 – Two Underground Rescue Squads 25

Chapter 4 – Made New in Old Saybrook, CT 29

Chapter 5 – Worked My Way into Prison
   - Kicked Out of Prison 33

Chapter 6 – Mount Monadnock, A Key National Portal
   in Past Years 37

Chapter 7 – Mean What You Say to God 41

Chapter 8 – Changing the Course of One's Life
   Is A Challenge 45

Chapter 9 – The Housewife's Hidden Dream, A Mysterious
   Mission in A Foreign Land 49

Chapter 10 – The Philippines Revolution and
   New President Cory Aquino 55

Chapter 11 – Breakthrough in Volcano and
   Vampire Bat Country 61

Chapter 12 – North Past Baguio City into
   Unknown Territory 65

Chapter 13 – "I'm Just Doing My Job,"
   God Does the Rest 70

Chapter 14 – A Place of "Honour" At the
Mountain Retreat 73

Chapter 15 – Strict Obedience Is Honoured 80

Chapter 16 – Comprehend the Essence and Interpret Your Past
Through God's Eyes 85

Chapter 17 – Walking Where the Lord Walked
in Person 88

Chapter 18 – Conclusion - Know Where the Power Is !....... 92

To the Reader,

I pray this little book can add spark to a day that is dark

...Can bring life to a dead dream....

...Can restore what seems to be no more...

...The lovely thing that was hidden in the heart.

Do not give up until you find out who you really are!

...And are able to enjoy it.

God will help you.

He is waiting for you to ask.

Me with my grandchildren.

Why are you about to read this little book?

Each story has a miracle of some kind.

And a message for the reader to interpret as they will.

Each story sends a prayer that you will never think it is too late, or that you are not adequate, to find your highest path, and your greatest goal.

Your greatest goal may be the simplest thing, *even a hidden thing*, and often is.

What you may need to realize is that you have indeed met goals and were not aware of it.

Or, you may need to realize that you have talents and skills which you did not know about.

That thing you always secretly wanted to do may be God wanting you to branch out; or dig in.

Since we all go through seasons in life, we need to be able to discern which season we are in, and take hold of it.

"Ask, and you shall receive."

So many of us begin our lives with great thoughts of being important... of doing something that matters... of reaching a pinnacle of success in some way.

As our lives progress, we tend to get caught up in the needs of the day, the relationship issues, the need to earn a living, or other pressures which beset us.

Sometimes we are trapped, so to speak, by the needs of those close to us.

Decisions and roads taken, or not taken, which did not seem to be that important at that moment, may have totally directed our lives.

My heart wish, for those who read these stories about a housewife who went from depression to adventure, is that each person who reads them will find their true destiny, joy, and know their true goals.

My other wish is that every reader will find others who share the same, or similar, loves, and desires, and goals. May you find others to share and help your vision.

"The fellowship of kindred minds (as the old anthem says) is like to that above."

Your journey may begin with music and end up in art. It may begin with business and end up as teaching. It may begin as a loner and end up adopting children... or from a bad student to a CEO.

May your horizons be expanded, and your hopes elevated as you read.

*Discovering beauty is exciting;
even in a field of sweet peas.*

> *Psalm 139:9-10*
>
> "If I take the wings of the morning,
>
> and dwell in the uttermost parts of the sea;
>
> Even there shall Thy Hand lead me,
>
> and Thy Right Hand shall hold me."

We may all be asking the same question!

How do these amazing things come to pass in a person's life? I am amazed as I write these adventures. Is it because we have done something right? ...I guess not!

I was a wild, insecure, young woman, living single in New York City–need I say more?

But! I was raised from the dead in New York Hospital, and then told I would never have children because I had experienced a rupture of a main artery by a fetus in one of my fallopian tubes and I had bled to death.

The operating room attendant said, "JESUS!...There is no blood pressure," and they pulled a green oilcloth over my head. I said, "I am not dead."

They gasped.

It was a miracle! I had no blood. Why was I alive? Certainly there was no logical reason. Did God know how my heart would respond, when it was the right time? My mother and grandmother prayed, and we went to the Methodist church. But, everyone was doing these "things" in New York! … "nice" people.

Still, I wondered if there was a reason why I was not dead.

I remembered when I was 18, and went bar-hopping in that city. We laughed and said we would "try out" the Billy Graham meeting at Madison Square Garden. I remembered that suddenly something powerful pulled me down to say some kind of prayer. But, now I was 27.

Then, I remembered when I was young, and I felt I had to walk alone out on the far sand bar at Chatham, on Cape Cod, and an enveloping cloud came on me, with the greatest peace.

I remember when a man mysteriously was present when I fell through the ice as a foolish child in a deserted pond, and he threw me a rope. Grandpa had told me the pond was twenty feet deep. Was it an angel?

But, surely this could not mean I was important to God! I went back to my wayward ways.

Three children later, to show God's mercy, (for I had only one fallopian tube), I hit a deep depression. The first child was three when the third was born. I happily nursed them all.

My husband, John, was frantically starting a newspaper business and I saw him maybe an hour a day. My big daily event was going to the grocery store, pushing two kids in one cart, and pulling one in the other.

Me with the kids at the beach.

I asked a psychiatrist if I would ever get better. He did not think so. Having noticed that he treated other women who were quite like me in a certain blasé manner, I stopped going to him.

My husband said, "Maybe you should try going to church." (I keep reminding him of this!).

So, God still had plans for me, and that church was ALIVE! ...with caring and praying women! My healing began and continues almost daily to this day, with my grateful appreciation.

Do you have some caring and praying friends? This is the heart of my calling–to help women find their destiny.

Everywhere God sent me, there was always a woman with the same heart. .

Does God have a plan for you? YES! ...A new one? CONSIDER what He has already done!

I had no funds, so He provided for every trip around the globe. Ask what He wants to do for you!

Me with my guitar at 76 years old.

Jeremiah 29:11

"For I know the thoughts that I think toward you, saith the LORD, thoughts of peace, and not of evil, to give you an expected end."

Chapter 1

GOD MOVED
IN THE ESTABLISHED CHURCH

I worked in the Episcopal bookstore in Providence, enjoying the atmosphere, as the Bishop, Frederick Belden, was a wonderful, wise, and fatherly man.

I also began to write, and the Episcopal newspaper published a few articles. One was entitled, "WHICH IS EASIER?", an exhortation toward the Scriptural understanding that both healing and salvation came in the same package from God at the Cross.

We are entitled to both.

A call came requesting my prayers for a small child who had been diagnosed with an inoperable brain tumor. A deacon drove me to her home to pray.

She was a beautiful little girl.

I took her face in my hands and looked into her eyes.

I said, "God did not give this to you; He wants you to be well."

She looked back at me with the trusting eyes of a child.

We received a report in a few days that the tumor was gone.

It was a miracle!

Another elder and his wife had a son who stopped on Route 95 to help someone and was hit by a speeding car. He was now in Boston, believed to be in a permanent vegetative state.

I called his father and asked if he wanted me to go and pray for his son.

His reply was that they had "tried everything else, so why not?"

I drove up to find his mother and sister sitting and watching a lifeless, unresponsive person. His head was bent over his chest and tubes, and wires were attached to him.

The Spirit led me to pray Ezekiel 37 out loud. It was the Scripture about speaking to the dry bones and telling them to rise up and to live again.

As I spoke these words, the young man slowly lifted his head. The miracle healing began.

His mother and sister were amazed…. It was the beginning of a strong faith walk for both of them. I handed them a cloth which had been prayed over by a strong ministry to transmit healing. His mother told me later that she held it many times to help with his healing.

Within a few weeks' time, the nurses began reporting that he was responding, sometimes lifting a hand. Needless to say, he is alive and functioning thanks to GOD and his family's prayers.

> **Romans 8:9 from the Passion Bible**
>
> "If anyone is not joined to the spirit of Christ, he cannot be himself."

Chapter 2

YOUR GIFTS
AND YOUR CALLINGS FROM GOD

We are born with certain capacities and talents and inherited tendencies. These can be anything from art to music, to math, to science, to business, to house organization, on through encouragement, etc. Once we realize what our "bent' is, it is up to us whether we pursue it, and then, whether it reaches the level it was intended to achieve. No matter what is in our way, if we are determined, we can find the level we seek in our inborn traits. It is our life, and our decision.

Carol Bo Howell

When my three children were small, I always stayed at home. Not only did I enjoy them, but no one else was going to bring them up! -- that is just how I was as a young mother. John would often ask, "Will you ever leave this house?" (Your story may be different, and that is OK).

I would see things. For instance, one day in my head I saw my daughter Diana reach for a piece of glass and put it in her mouth. I was outside but ran in to find her in her playpen next to a windowsill on which, not known to me, were pieces of glass! How God gives gifts to mothers!

Once I was in the water and my young children were with me having fun. I suddenly realized that Ted was not nearby. I went to look for him and found that he had turned upside down in the water in his life jacket and could not get back up. He could have drowned. (He is a wind surfer! God's hand is on him.)

My third child, Jack, was another story. We were visiting friends who lived on a deserted road. At some point I asked where Jack was. I was told not to be so "uptight," but I persisted. I went outside while all the gathering was having beer and headed toward the road. I could hear a car coming in the distance. Then I saw him running toward the road and looking back at me, over his shoulder, laughing, like this was a game! I ran and caught up with him, and actually tackled him just before he got to the road. (I was six months pregnant with Ted!)

That three year old is still a world traveler.

How could I ever have known I would be a "seer" after God got hold of me? There is more.

My grandmother, who had always been my best friend, was now 93. I kept in touch with her as much as possible for she had been the person who really believed in me. She always had a Bible next to her bed and was always helping people. Everyone loved her. She and Grandpa lived literally, "over the river and through the woods," so I spent a lot of time with them as a young person. I would go through the woods with my dog to visit them almost every day.

But now Mimi had received a bad report from the doctor. I got in the car with Diana, who was quite small, and we drove from Rhode Island to New York to see Mimi.

Mimi looked depressed, and at one point, she said to me, "I can't believe it is all over." (I had asked God, on the drive down, Who I did not know at all at that time, to give me the right words. Out of my mouth came these words: "It is not the end; it is just the beginning."

Now understand, please; I did not even believe this, and yet I spoke the words, -- before I could change them. God uses us when we are ignorant.

In all of these cases, God was giving me gifts before I knew what they were. He'll do it for you.

> "He led them about,
>
> He instructed them,
>
> He kept them as the Apple of His Eye."

Chapter 3

TWO UNDERGROUND RESCUE SQUADS

My friend's voice kept repeating these words from the back seat of the car, "This has to be love… This has to be love."

She was seated in between a tall Easter lily and my 82-pound Dobie-Shepherd mix, named "Binky." Binky was named by someone who had not taken a good look at the tall black dog. My friend had come to help, for I had made one three-and-a-half-hour trip after another to try to follow up on Aunt Catherine.

We were driving down the highway bringing Catherine home. My great aunt Catherine had been in a hospital which had decided no one wanted her to live. She was

93, and had been given no water or food for three days. The nurses had called and told me to take her home where we could give her food and drink. They had seen how feisty she was and that we cared. This is amazing.

Aunt Catherine's drawing of the mountains.

As we drove home, Catherine used her index finger to draw each mountain and tree that she could see out the window. She was a masterful artist and was delighted to form a fresh new painting in her mind. She also loved music, played the piano, and never missed listening to the Metropolitan Opera from New York every week. I had taken art lessons from her as a child and she was my Godmother. She had been "married" to her artwork alone, so I was her only relative.

My daughter had flown in from Wyoming to visit Catherine a few days before. An MPT, she had asked medical questions which made the hospital people think and realize we wanted Catherine to live. Aunt Catherine had also missed her evening "pick-up drink."

Aunt Catherine with my three children.

Now painting and listening to music in heaven, she has the pleasure of knowing that the monies which she left to me have paid for some excellent music CDs which have gone global -- even into the underground churches in China.

On the other side of the family, my husband John's aunt was diagnosed with more than a few very serious physical problems and was in the hospital in Connecticut.

All I had heard for days was that "she must be dead by now,"–with so many problems.

I called a friend of "the cloth," Sister Marguerite. She agreed to go with me to pray for Jean.

Sister Marguerite is "a trip" and would phone me every once in a while to say, "Get me out of here!" (She lived in a nunnery, and so we would go out to eat, or she would come to our home to visit.) She had an amazing gift to teach children about God.

When we got to the hospital, Jean had just come out of the OR, and we were told we could not go in. But Sister Marguerite marched into the ICU as was her "habit!" I just followed… she knew what she was doing! We put our hands on Jean's feet and prayed. She responded. Jean went home, healed. At one family gathering in the next year or so, Jean said, "Thanks for the prayer!" A "miracle."

Chapter 4
MADE NEW IN OLD SAYBROOK

"The next train to Providence is at 1 p.m." The man behind the ticket booth at the train station in Old Saybrook gave me the information I needed.

The Episcopal Charismatic Movement was going strong, and this was a conference led by Rev. Terry Fulham, their kingpin. It was 1975.

I had left my three little children at home and had come with some friends who were very active priests in Rhode Island. I was amazed to see all the happy people holding hands and dancing around the church and I wanted to join in.

My husband had asked me to come home after one day so I was finding out how to get home by train. Therefore, by 1 p.m. I was back at the train station. We waited and waited, but there was no train. I went in to ask the man behind the ticket counter, but it was not the same man. He informed me that there was no 1 p.m. train to Providence!

God wanted me to stay!

Amazed, we went back to the conference where they were preaching about the Baptism of The Holy Spirit. I was desperate for anything God wanted to give to me, having been through some time of depression. I had not eaten (and thought I might die) but when The Love of God poured down through me like liquid gold, life was changed. This was the real thing!

I cried for three days, just from the Power and Presence of that love.

When I finally arrived home to the family, my husband was not sure about the train story. I even had a "visitation" from a neighboring man I hardly knew who came into my house and shouted at me for leaving my children.

At one point, I knelt beside my bed and asked The Lord, "IS that all there is?"

His Presence came so strongly that I could not breathe and I said, "OK, I believe You Lord."

Because of this glorious experience, I immediately went to the nursing homes, prisons, and hospitals with my guitar. (I had tried to learn to play the guitar but could not do so until I had received this anointing from God). He had given me that skill, with a new song from Psalm 92, when I was in the motel in Old Saybrook.

I did not receive my personal message from The Holy Spirit right away. It came months later when a lovely praise team visited our church, along with one simple prophetic word: "Peace."

I often had to call a friend on the phone and ask her to pray in The Spirit so that I could keep my prayer language going. Finally it could flow like the river of living water Jesus spoke about. (John 4:14)

God uses anyone who desires Him to move through them. But this was my own experience.

Psalm 92:12-15 -

"The righteous shall flourish like a palm tree,

and grow like a cedar in Lebanon.

Planted in the house of The Lord,

they shall flourish in the Courts of our God.

They shall still bring forth fruit in old age;

they shall be full of sap and green.

The show that The Lord is upright;

He is my Rock,

and there is no unrighteousness in Him."

Chapter 5
WORKED MY WAY INTO THE PRISON– KICKED OUT OF THE PRISON

I could not drive by the Rhode Island State Prison without wondering how many inmates in there did not deserve to be locked up.

One day, I decided to see if I could go in and play my guitar and try to somehow cheer people up.

My home church said I had to take a three-year course and get a large cross before I could go in. But I found a Catholic nun who wanted help, and who was doing a great work in the prisons.

The problem was that I had to go through an Episcopal chaplain who was not happy about my attempts, or what she termed my "extreme" enthusiasm. But finally, she called me on the phone and said that she had not slept for a week, and so I could now go in. The Lord makes the way.

I had been going into the locked wards of the mental institutions every week for seven years. Just going every week, singing, and loving the people had shown results by emptying one of the worst wards.

A few examples of my welcomes:

One lady would urinate on the floor every time I came to sing. Another would sneak up behind me, breathing heavily, like a hissing, while the attendants took a break. One lady shouted, "Get the hell out of here." My response was, "That is just what I am trying to do." She paused, thought about it, and walked out.

But the big day was when I went into the locked women's prison ...I had been okayed to be their Sunday chaplain.

Hearing the many locks clang shut behind me, I held my guitar and then I heard the Scripture, "For this I was born, and for this I came into the world."

So, ...Onward! ...Cast out the fearful thoughts.

What a rewarding although totally exhausting experience.

The ones who wanted to hear the good news came. So many had been skillfully misused, to take the hit for others. Some women were just trying to feed their family, the wrong way. Some had killed, and some where accused wrongly of killing.

"Nice" people would ask me how I could enjoy being with the prisoners.

I gave them a simple prayer–"Jesus is the door; Jesus has the keys; and Jesus lives in me."

There were times when I felt I actually preferred them, for there were many good hearts which had been turned bad by life's very hard things, and they wanted to change for the better.

Some would appear before the judge who had originally put them in prison and would be set free, for even the judge could see that they were changed people. God had done good work.

I began to get calls from around the country, saying, "I am still doing good!"

My work was not appreciated by everyone, especially those who felt the women should still be punished for their full term. When I told my husband, he said, "Is that not what it is all about?... Change?"

As a consequence, the prison attendant created a reason to kick me out of prison. They found mouthwash in my bag.

One door shuts; another door opens..

Chapter 6

MOUNT MONADNOCK - A KEY NATIONAL PORTAL IN PAST YEARS

This part of New Hampshire was now an area where God was moving by His Grace through small but strong meetings, both in homes and in the old churches, which seemed to speak of history and smelled old, like they remembered some things we need to know.

We were gathered in a large home on a hill near this mountain, Monadnock.

A number of interested people, mostly intercessors, had come to seek The Lord, to hear God's Word, and to worship together.

I had a special attachment to this mountain because all of my three children had climbed to the top as part of school bus trips from Rhode Island. I had gone each time to make the climb.

It is not a huge mountain, but well-travelled, even somehow beloved. Apparently there is a portal importance there in the global time clock.

The Spirit had told me to teach on Ephesians 4 in which the apostle Paul speaks of the strong importance of putting off the "old man" and putting on the "new man." Apparently, as we seek and find The Lord, we can, by The Spirit of God, assist Him in changing the unsavory parts of our personality into what He had created us to be.

The same message is given by the apostle Paul in Colossians Chapter 3, and in Galatians 3... the need for our putting off the old personality, and putting on the new, by the power of The Spirit.

We were all interested in this change, and after the message was finished, we began to pray. God began to join with us, and soon we were totally energized in our prayers and music.

As the meeting was drawing to a close, a friend began to blow her shofar (ram's horn) and we all gave a huge shout.

We went home happy.

But, the next morning we were startled by the national news.

The famous Old Man of The Mountain up north of us had fallen down during the night !

Some girl scouts were climbing early that morning and had discovered the rubble. New Hampshire was rocked!

A friend from D.C. called me and said, "I know you were there!"...It is still a mystery! Where is the "new man"?

Me with Sandy and her shofar.

Habakkuk 1:5

"Behold, among the heathen, and regard,

and wonder marvelously:

For I will do a work in your days which you will

not even believe, though it be told to you."

Chapter 7
MEAN WHAT YOU SAY TO GOD

The preacher at Zion Bible Institute in Rhode Island was reciting a verse from Isaiah 6:8 in which the prophet says to God, "Here I am. Send me."

I was drawn to the front of the church and ended up on the floor at the speaker's feet.

I went home, and every morning, took the phone off the hook to study God's Word while my three children were at school.

How could I have known that three years later, I would start a new adventure with God? For I had said, "Send me."

Then a radio preacher to whom I avidly listened every day announced that he was going to take a group to the Philippines for a mission trip.

My heart jumped; but I said, "Lord, I know you want me home with my growing children... BUT ... if you want me to go on this trip, please let me know."

A typical Filipino village.

Within a week a wealthy business friend called and asked me the question, "What do you need?" I told him the amount, and he brought it to me.

Church and related people told me I should not leave my family for this trip. The Lord assured me that HE would take care of my husband and children ... they might even enjoy the change!

A typical market.

As the plane crossed the Pacific during the 14 hour crossing, there was much laughter in the team. The leaders, who were well-known ministers, seemed to know that this was a good sign. The stewardesses were not so sure, seeing that some of us were lying on the floor in laughter.

The huge meetings were strong; but the real fun was walking in Luneta Park with my guitar.

On one such walk, I noticed about fifty men huddled in a circle. They were squatting, and the leader wore a leather strip around his neck with some sort of thing hanging down from it.

The two men who were walking the park with me thought we should move on quickly.

I agreed, but felt I should check in The Word about those men.

To my surprise, a Scripture was highlighted which said, "He went and stood among them".

Could that be for me? A woman? I decided I needed to take the faith stance and go.

As I approached, the leader stood up very slowly and looked at me carefully. Then the man said, "Can you help us? We were discussing salvation."

My two male friends came back and led the men to The Lord, Who is Trustworthy and Faithful. He was answering their heart.

When I arrived home, my husband, who was against this trip, said he got to know his children while I was gone. God has his ways.

Chapter 8

CHANGING THE COURSE OF ONE'S LIFE IS A CHALLENGE

I was seated at the long dining room table which sat about twelve people. Until that very moment, I was very much accepted in this family group.

Then I mentioned that I would soon take a missionary trip to the Philippine Islands.

A fist slammed down on the table sending wine and water glasses jumping and bringing all who were eating to sharp attention. The man of the house next to me said, "You will come back a corpse!" To be fair, the patriarch of this family knew exactly what was happening in the Philippines because of business connections, and that a revolution was probably coming. However, this proclamation with his fist was not received by me as a blessed send-off.

My conversion to Christianity was a shock to many, for my past history read otherwise. But if we consider Bible history, not many were so great when The Hound of Heaven got hold of them.

My grandfather on my mother's side was George Garrison Backhouse, and he was a captain in the U.S. Calvary in Galveston, Texas.

Three photos from my grandfather's time in the cavalry.

Captain Grandpa Backhouse.

As I consider my calling, it is very similar to my grandfather's -- guarding boundaries and patrolling places where God is working, as well as surrounding people in prayers through whom God is planning to work. It is called intercession.

The Bible prophets, especially Zechariah, often mention those on horseback whom God sends to certain places of tumult. And when they go and obey His Voice, we read that His Spirit can be put at rest in that place by their obedience.

"Thy Way is in the sea, and Thy path in the great waters, and Thy footsteps are not known." Psalm 77:19.

Many of us, who may consider our lives to be " not much of import" will be very surprised when we meet in heaven to find that a simple thing we did, or said, or even modelled… which did not seem important at the time… has changed lives, even history. I believe there will be wonderful videos in heaven which will reveal what we each did, as the poet said, leaving our "Footsteps in the sands of time." Henry Wadsworth Longfellow.

Chapter 9

THE HOUSEWIFE'S HIDDEN DREAM
A MYSTERIOUS MISSION
IN A FOREIGN LAND

I woke up in Antipolo, Philippines, with the sense of a mission.

I was in the home of two American missionaries, Chuck and Joan Dewing, and this was prior to the Filipino revolution, which resulted with Cory Acquino becoming the new president in Manila.

I knew I had to go to the bus station down the hill at 4 p.m. I told the Dewing's my plan, and we prayed.

The bus station was alive with "jeepneys" which were old American army jeeps converted into small busses. These colorfully decorated vehicles would take chickens, pigs, produce, and people. The people were usually jammed in, seated hip to hip; but everyone was always happy.

A 1980s Jeepney in Manila

I got on the bus which was to take me to a place whose name was unrecognizable, for the sign on the front of the bus was written in lengthy Tagalog language.

But I did not know where I would end up by the end of the day, so that was fine.

Over hills and through little villages, with chickens and pigs and a singing driver, we bounced and swerved. I was hearing my own songs as well (and I am wondering now if it was angels rejoicing at my adventure).

As it grew darker, we came into a small village on the side of a large lagoon. I heard The still small Voice urging me to get off.

Men were wandering into town leading water buffalo and carrying large sickles for threshing. I stood in the rough square holding my little red Bible against my chest and praying.

Shortly thereafter, a lovely looking Filipino woman walked quietly up to me and said these words – "We have been waiting for you; the pastor is over there." God had spoken to them about me.

She pointed to a nice-looking man who had a scooter with a side car.

Totally amazed, I went with them along the dirt paths to their church which was a grass hut with a cement floor. (I can still smell, with nice remembrance, the smoldering bamboo air which was simple fuel the Filipinos used to cook their family meals.)

My friend who gave me a place to sleep.

They urged me to give them a message, and I was ready to speak encouragement and Scriptural teaching. (I had been taught to be "instant... in season and out.")

The people were so happy to hear good things from an American... and I was so happy to be there.

I spent the night in a hanging, mosquito-netted bed with this sweet woman, (mosquitoes being kept outside). And in the morning, she put me on the bus back to the Manila area.

There is no end to the adventures our Lord can bring us when we learn to trust His leading.

Pastor Ben Mutia

Proverbs 3:5-6

Trust in the LORD with all thine heart;
and lean not unto thine own understanding.
In all thy ways acknowledge him,
and he shall direct thy paths.

Isaiah 45:8

Rain down, you heavens, from above,

and let the skies pour down righteousness;

let the earth open,

and let them bring forth salvation,

and let righteousness spring up together.

I, The Lord, have created It."

Chapter 10

THE PHILIPPINE REVOLUTION
AND NEW PRESIDENT CORY AQUINO

My long Northwest flight landed safely in Manila. It was the first plane to land following the revolution.

Knowing that Cory Aquino's husband had been recently murdered in that very airport, I was a bit concerned. But God had promised me safety. It seemed that The Lord was on my right hand and the angel Michael at my left.

After getting through customs, I walked out into the hot and crowded city street with a maze of brown faces watching all who had landed. As usual, I was not sure who would meet me when I came out, since mail took two weeks each way. (I thus sent my itinerary to a few people, just in case.)

But there was Chuck Dewing! He patiently and cheerfully led me from smelly bus to smelly bus and on to their home in Antipolo, Rizal, lugging my suitcase, which preceded today's wheels.

A church in Antipolo.

As can often be the case, the real and spectacular stories about the revolution were not printed in the newspapers. Chuck took me to speak with the men who were in the middle of the fray so that I could write my little book and show the truth of the revolution -- which was that God did it!

Christians had laid down in the streets to block tanks. Massive prayer had covered Malacañang Palace so that when the hordes of people rushed in after the Marcos' left, not one of the hundreds of bombs went off! (All of these bombs were later detonated after the people were moved out, with greatest caution and amazement.) It was miraculous.

President Corazon (Cory) Aquino.

The two men closest to Mrs. Aquino, like herself, were believers. The nation had been bathed in prayers. After she became president, she arranged for all her staff to take the "Life in The Spirit seminar", a wonderful Catholic teaching.

She was an amazing woman, and realized that she was an interim answer. She took the time to answer two handwritten notes I had sent to her with great respect on my part, as a hopeful encouragement to her, and she answered with her own handwriting.

One true story from the revolution is worth the rendering here:

A pilot left his home in the morning during the revolution. He ordered his wife to stay in the house all day, knowing what his orders were. He was commanded to fly over the protesters and to fire on the crowds.

As the plane descended to do this job, he saw the face of his wife and could not fire. This was repeated several times, and each time he saw her and could not fire.

When he got home, he asked her why she went out of the house against his request.

God can make people see what they need to see. Her reply was that she never left.

(There were also several times when the clouds of tear gas were mysteriously blown away from the praying crowds.)

May this encourage us to do what is right in our own nation in these troubled times. Here are a few Scriptures to pray for our own nation, and the Capitol in Washington -

---

Isaiah 1:26

"I will restore your judges as at the first,
and your counselors as at the beginning.
You shall be called the City of Righteousness,
the faithful city."

Isaiah 9:7

"Of the increase of His government
and of His peace there will be no end"
"...to order it and establish it,
with judgment and justice,
from this time forward,
even henceforth and forever.

The Zeal of The Lord of Hosts will perform this."

> *Proverbs 24:27 Amplified Version*
>
> "(Put first things first,);
> Prepare your work outside,
> And get it ready for yourself in the field;
>
> And afterward build your house
> and establish a home."

Chapter 11

BREAKTHROUGH IN VOLCANO AND VAMPIRE BAT COUNTRY

When Pastor Larry from Laguna, Philippines, asked me to go with him on an important mission, I knew that meant "important."

Having been a guest preacher in his church in Laguna during a number of years of mission trips, I knew the man and his family, and their integrity. Larry had started other churches in the Philippines as well, and was a father to them all.

We started out on a scooter which was the normal way to travel through the Filipino countryside.

The first night we each slept on boards in an open church yard accompanied by wild rats which he occasionally took by the tail and threw out of the church when they began chewing on the boards.

By the second day we were on pathways and on foot, visiting his founded churches on the way. Our mission was to a brother pastor who had started a church in a very dangerous area of the volcano country. His life was constantly threatened, and he did not dare to have his wife and children join him in such conditions.

A water buffalo in volcano territory.

We walked carefully through a small village which had an atmosphere that was almost tangibly dark. Relieved to get through, we then came to the grass hut which was the church of this young pastor. His bed was a woven rectangular part which hung out from the rest of the building. That was his life.

I was to deliver the message for the meeting. I spoke of the power of the Holy Spirit, for we realized that if his people got hold of the authority of this Gift, they would be able to help carry the pastor through to victory. He needed a congregation to support and work with him.

After the message, the entire group received the Holy Spirit and there was great joy.

There were about fifty Filipinos crowded into that small grass-roofed church.

Sensing that we had done what was needed, we headed out for home.

As we arrived back at the village which had seemed so dark, we were startled to see a body in the street, and blood. At this point a very angry young man with a large knife came toward me. He obviously thought I was the cause of the trouble, or wanted to make me, a white person, the cause.

When he started toward me, out of my mouth came these words:
"In The Name of Jesus... "

I could get no further, but that was apparently all that was needed. The man stopped in his tracks, and froze with the knife in his hand. The Lord has frozen him in place.

We made a quick exit and walked faster through the village and sighed with relief to go on our way. At this point, a large water buffalo suddenly came after us. (Now we were running!). But God was faithful again. We finally got to our scooter on foot and then went on our way to our homes. (I was very relieved to return to the home of my missionary friends in Antipolo, Rizal, but I was also excited about the deliverance for the young pastor. I was even more excited about the protection of God... He had spoken the powerful Name of Jesus through my mouth for me.)

It was a miraculous deliverance from injury or death.

Chapter 12

NORTH PAST BAGUIO CITY, INTO UNKNOWN TERRITORY

l could not look out the window. We had just passed the highest point on the island of Luzon, Philippines. The bus was careening down a steep road, and there was a feeling of chaos.

The driver, however, had done this many times before and was quite cheerful. Maybe he was born for this.

Chuck Dewing had planned a series of meetings for me to speak in a remote place called Benguet. He had indulgently billed me as an American evangelist. pastors were walking for days to be part of this event.

He smiled as he looked out the window of the noisy bus, having survived many such trips. The situation at the time was serious, as apparently, the Communist Chinese were picking off pastors, mayors, and journalists in these remote parts of the islands.

As we approached a valley which looked like a picture postcard of a peaceful resort, we realized it was our destination. It was a jewel which I can still see.

Benguet church.

I was relieved to notice that the pastor had every book written by one of my favorite authors, E.W. Kenyon.

His wife, however, had a large, black pet spider that I encountered in the middle of the night when I visited the outdoor latrine. Not knowing it was her pet, I had swiped at it in the dark, but was amazed to see it look back at me as if to say, 'What are you doing?" I feared it might be poisonous.

But she brought him out on her finger the next morning at breakfast to introduce him to me formally.

As the people began to arrive, I spent a lot of time preparing in the church itself, which was an old metal dome from the war. Surprised, I noticed that very few thought of joining me in prayer. The shocker to them was that God had instructed me to teach on prayer.

It did not seem to be significant to them that when they asked for rain, I prayed and God sent it -- that day-- and when they asked to pray for it to stop, it stopped -- that very day! Even I was amazed as we saw Him work these things. He was showing them the power of prayer.

"But where is this wild and exciting evangelist?"

(Persistent, God knew what they really needed to survive was to understand the power of prayer). Apparently, this fact did not enter their mind, and soon the pastor decided to bring up a person from town to speak to them about... birth control... replacing me, and my message.

At one of my next meetings, The Lord began to rebuke them, and then I asked them why no one came to pray with me... for their prayers may have made the meetings take another turn.

Then, since my "replacement" had not arrived from town, I went up to work the last meeting. It was dusk; and I became aware of subdued faces, arriving quietly, and joining me in prayer.

After the message, I asked if anyone would like the laying on of hands for prayer. The people came forward. Chuck had come up and was going to minister beside me.

Then a portal of Glory opened over us! When I prayed for a person, they would flip into the air and land back somewhere else. Fortunately, Chuck was there to remind me that this really did happen. It was not something I made up and could write on a postcard to send back home.

It was God's own power on exhibition. Needless to say, God broke into that meeting in a glorious way.

Apparently, I was to teach on prayer–they were to pray–and He Himself was to be The Evangelist…

We were all satisfied!

John 14:15- taken from The Passion Bible

"Loving Me empowers you to obey My commands"

…The words of Jesus.

Chapter 13

"I'M JUST DOING MY JOB" GOD DOES THE REST

This phrase became a happy ice breaker in my future mission trips, especially in Russia where "doing your job" can be a fanatical and often impractical thing.

For this Filipino "job," Pastor Carlos Obana had cleared his family out of their double bed and placed it in the church for me. It was normal for whole families to share a bed in the Philippines, and so this was a great honor that churches without large funds could give to a guest.

As I prepared in my "special plot," I knew I had to teach on healing. The fact that my face was now covered with red mosquito bites was not pertinent.

The Obana family.

The Obana's had told neighbors about this meeting. The little church was full... bed and all.

(The Filipinos were usually so hungry toward God, and ready to receive, that answers to prayer were way beyond one's own normal ministry to heal. In one such street meeting, where people were holding onto my legs in the dark, a woman began to shriek. She then began to bare her breast in order to show us all that a tumor had just fallen off). A miracle!

With this "under my belt," I began the healing service.

I gave Scripture and some proof of testimonies... that it is God's will and desire to heal. The people were attentive.

Then I asked them to come up for prayer if they so desired. Most of them came forward.

To my surprise, there was absolutely no indication of healings, for anyone.

I gulped, and taught them that God watches over His Word to perform it, and He will meet them.

As I flew home, I hoped I had responded the right way and had done what The Lord wanted.

(There is always that unkind suggestion that wants us to wonder what we did wrong. I had to keep remembering that it is God, and not me, Who heals.)

Two weeks later I received a letter from Pastor Carlos. (It took two weeks for mail to arrive from the Philippines at that time.)

He reported that everyone was healed!

Hmm ... Did The Lord want them to know that He Himself could heal them, whether the American minister was there or not? God is the miracle worker!

Isaiah 50:4

"The Lord God has given to me

the tongue of the learned,

That I should know how to speak a Word in

Season to those that are weary;

He wakens me morning by morning,

He wakens my ear to hear as the learned."

Chapter 14

A PLACE OF HONOUR AT THE MOUNTAIN RETREAT

"And we will have a special place for you to sleep at our mountain retreat."

Pastor Evelyn Mangampo had asked me to speak at a retreat in the hills of Luzon Island, Philippines, and it sounded wonderful to me.

We headed out on foot into the remote places, my guitar on my back. I was an "easy read" on this happy trek as an American, or at least a foreigner, with fair hair and lighter skin.

As the path got narrower and narrower, we would walk beneath elevated grass homes. These warm people are so eager to be social that some families had actually built their homes in trees over the dirt pathway so that they would not miss anyone walking through. Big smiles greeted me through the thick green vegetation saying, "American, American." It was delightful.

An elevated grass home built over a path.

Some hours later, we arrived at the site for the retreat. About seventy eager people were already there, along with their chickens. It was a raised platform of about fifty feet in diameter with a "form" of a sound system.

As it grew dark, I asked for the latrine.

Sister Mangampo then took the microphone, and with great force and delight in her use of the English language said, " Seesterr Carrolle shall now urrinnaate."

Me with Sister Evelyn Mangampo

The people all looked with great interest as she led me off to the side of the platform to some nearby bushes, apparently just for me. With that situation being resolved, the meeting began with music which even the chickens enjoyed. They loved the meeting, preening, sitting among the people, and being stroked as I spoke. (I had my chance to pat the "cluckers" during the music.)

At the close of the meeting, Sister M told the people in their Tagalog language (she was my interpreter), to prepare to sleep. They laid down in rows on the platform, side by side, like a well-organized garden just covering the floor. Then she took some colorful scarves out, with great pride, and carefully arranged them in the center of the group in the shape of a coffin.

My ministry.

With great pomp she indicated that this was my place of rest.

We were all blessed, and all slept well... even the chickens. How wonderful, how simple, and so free!

What would we do without a sense of humor? "A merry heart worketh good, like medicine."

A typical mountain church

Considering that there was no telephone access, computer, post office, or even any knowledge of where I was, The Goodness of God is of even greater notice.

Just a sense of God's Pleasure and prayers of friends, family, and a love for these gentle and enthusiastic people made it work.

Note - Mrs. Mangampo had ten children, no teeth, and lived in a small grass hut–but was so HAPPY.

Isaiah 6:8 Amplified Version

"Also I heard The Voice of The Lord, saying,

'Whom shall I send?

And who will go for Us?

Then, said I,

"Here am I:

send me.".

Chapter 15

STRICT OBEDIENCE IS HONOURED

"YOU HAVE BEEN DISOBEDIENT!" The prophet's finger was pointing at me from the platform. I uttered a wail, to my surprise, and then fell backward.

How could this be? The ministry I was with was to leave the Philippines and then fly the very next day to South Africa. Surely I had to get home to my husband and children! It would be school vacation week, and I had to be there with them.

But no, I was to go home for one day and take off again! (Little did I know that this year the vacation week would be changed... just in time.) A seeming miracle.

A view from the road in South Africa.

The flight to South Africa is long with a stop in the black and barren Azore Island airport.
But the meetings, which were held in a church which was used by the late John G. Lake, were warmly alive and wonderful. Intercession in his prayer room behind the podium was such that I had never experienced before. By The Holy Spirit, I was simultaneously speaking in prayer what the minister was preaching out front. The anointing was still alive there in that prayer room!

At these meetings, I was asked to travel down south through the Karoo region and speak on prayer in the home churches.

God moved mightily in these various home meetings, which then ended up in Port Elizabeth in a lively Episcopal Church. The people were so gracious. Seeing the same flowers that we grow here in New England was such a blessing since it was wintertime at home.

A lovely couple escorted me to the airport. I was seated with a young woman who was going to be married to an American man when she arrived in the USA. She was explaining to me the difference between black, white, and colored people in South African thinking. I then knew why some people looked at us strangely as we were having such a good time together.

At the stop in the Azores, there was a surprisingly long delay and we all began to get nervous. We were told that they were working on the plane. More delay. We all paced... I prayed.

Walking Where God Walks

Finally, we were told we could board the aircraft. We then just sat on the tarmac. Now I was instructed by The Holy Spirit to play praise music. Nervously, I turned it on. People were stoic. I played the whole tape.

Then I was told to stand up and pray for the plane! Yikes! People shifted their legs and remained stoic.

Finally we took off for home. I asked an attendant what had been wrong, and how wonderful that they were able to fix it!

His response: "It was the hydraulic system. There were no repairmen." It was a miracle!

The view from the window on that flight.

John 5:19 King James Version (KJV)

Then answered Jesus and said unto them, Verily, verily, I say unto you, The Son can do nothing of himself, but what he seeth the Father do: for what things soever he doeth, these also doeth the Son likewise.

Chapter 16

COMPREHEND THE ESSENCE AND INTERPRET YOUR PAST THROUGH GOD'S EYES

Some experiences are unpleasant when they happen; but in retrospect, God can bring forth a good thing (and a very important personal revelation) out of what seemed bad which we need to comprehend. Such clarity came to me from a time in the early 1990's in Colorado.

I was ministering several meetings at Resurrection Fellowship on the "call" of the watchman, as stated in Ezekiel Chapter 33, about the power of the night watch to break through regions.

There had been a miracle already–I was scheduled to lead an intimate Sunday evening meeting, not held in the large sanctuary, and I had announced this series of meetings in the various morning services.

When evening came, I was there with my guitar and the message. To our surprise, the place filled up with more than 500 people. The pastor asked, "who is doing music, the message?" It was me, as Jesus led.

We worshipped, and the specific Word went forth. During the morning service, the pastor had given me a prophetic word about "apostolic prayer," and as he said, "whatever that means."

At the close of the meeting, it was revealed that many people had been driving down the major north-south route on which this church was situated and had been told, or led, to turn into our meeting. It was obviously a supernatural meeting.

But here is the negative side, or so it has seemed, until now, when God gave me "eyes to see."

I had always wanted to own a motorcycle, and the husband of my friend had one. He offered to pick me up at one of the church meetings and drive me back to their home. I was excited.

I jumped on the small seat behind him and he took off. No instruction, no help–he just took off. As we were heading toward the highway, I figured I should take hold of the low handle in front of me. Then he accelerated to eighty and began to weave wildly in and out of the many sixteen-wheelers on the road. By now I had put my arms around his waist and just held on "for dear life." I was shaken.

For years, this memory has tried to trigger animosity toward this man who did not seem to care what happened to me, or even respect the breakthrough ministry I was trying to bring to his church.

But a moment in prayer showed me that this was a prophetic picture of God's total care and protection.

What has seemed to be negative treatment in my life has turned into praise to a faithful God.

Chapter 17

WALKING WHERE THE LORD WALKED IN PERSON

In my younger years, I often prayed right through the night and it actually often gave me more energy than if I had slept. My pastor Bernice Perry and I spent many nights praying in the Rhode Island area, and I continued to do so on the mission fields.

In the Philippines, I prayed nights for President Cory Aquino and she actually thanked me, for it was in the time of the revolution.

In one of those nights, I heard a voice telling me to go to Russia. I quickly cast it out of my mind, -- but it did not leave. The thought was frightening to me, and so when my friends took a mission trip to Russia, I stayed in Jerusalem and prayed for them from there.

I actually thought I was safer praying alone there– which is ridiculous!

Carol at the ancient synagogue at Capernaum

Little did I know that I would soon make 34 trips to Russian-speaking nations to help with large city-wide music festivals. I am so glad I did not miss this amazing experience. We saw whole cities which had experienced great anti-Semitic persecution totally transformed by the beautiful music and dancing... there was never any admission fee. Thousands were eternally changed.

But in the meantime, I stayed and prayed alone at a little house on the Mount of Olives in a Muslim neighborhood.

One morning, as I was walking out on the small grassy area, I realized that there was a gully that led down into the garden of Gethsemane to my right. How miraculous that this same rugged pathway is the very same one Jesus took on the donkey as He was going into His Palm Sunday experience!

It has not changed.

Walking where God walks is a Gift. He wants it for every one of His Own.

A good way to understand this loving and protective side of God is to imagine yourself as a parent, grabbing the hand of your child to make sure they get safely and securely across the street.
It is never too late for you!

Caleb took his promised mountain at the age of eighty.

> Let us, then, be up and doing,
> Hold God's hand in every case.
> Still perceiving, still pursuing,
> Learn to labor; use your faith.

---

1 CORINTHIANS 2:9-10

But as it is written, Eye hath not seen, nor ear heard, neither have entered into the heart of man, the things which God hath prepared for them that love him.

¹But God hath revealed them unto us by his Spirit: for the Spirit searcheth all things, yea, the deep things of God.

Chapter 18

CONCLUSION: KNOW WHERE THE POWER IS!

Can you go beyond your own mind and work wonders?

As it is written, "eye has not seen, nor ear heard, neither have entered into the heart of man, the things which God has prepared for them that love Him."

"But God has revealed them unto us by His Spirit: for The Spirit searches all things, yes, the deep things of God…"

"…now we have received not the spirit of the world, but The Spirit Which Is of God: that we might know the things that are freely given to us of God."

1 Corinthians 2:9,10,12, KJV, from Isaiah 64:4-7. (Please read 1 Cor.2 in the amplified version.)

The prophet Isaiah goes on to say that those who "receive and know" are the ones who call on His Name and who will "stir up themselves to take hold of Him." The Spirit and The Word are two doorways into revelation, and into living above man's systems.

The prophet Habakkuk also encourages us in chapter 1:5, saying, "Behold among the nations and regard, and wonder marvelously, for I, (God), will work a work in your days, which you will not believe, though it be told you."

As we see above, the wonders of God can only be comprehended, made manifest, or even observed by The Work of the Holy Spirit. Is there anyone who does not need this gift?

Habakkuk goes on in chapter three to give us hope by prophesying that God WILL come and revive His

Work "in the midst of the years," and even in wrath, will remember His great Mercy.

The prophet Jeremiah, even in the midst of the gloom and destruction that he is forced to see, speaks this amazing statement about the signs and wonders God can perform.

God, who is "great in counsel and mighty in Word, who has SET signs and wonders in the land of Egypt, even unto THIS day, AND in Israel, AND among other men" is still able to make a people a "name" at THIS day.

Like the promised Rest of God, this ability to perform miracles, signs, and wonders is still not only available, but is Father God's deep desire... now AT THIS DAY we are living in!

The prophet Joel also prophesied this ability and gifting for mankind, and then Peter spoke it forth on the Day of Pentecost proving Joel's words. When all the people in Jerusalem heard the words of God in their own native tongue from the mouths of the believers, it was proof that The Spirit had indeed been "poured out on ALL flesh," with a "Mighty Rushing Wind."

As all peoples can now see the defilement, greed, and ugliness which is trying to take over this planet. More than ever, God's lovers need to exhibit His powerful signs, wonders, and miracles.

Lord God, show us how to prepare, believe, and walk in this signal path which leads to reviving.

A big present-day global miracle is the mass returning of the Jewish people to their homeland (Aliyah). This was prophesied over 365 times for the "last days" in the Old Testament.

Hebrews 11:6

"But without faith it is impossible to please him: for he that cometh to God must believe that he is, and that he is a rewarder of them that diligently seek him."

From Deuteronomy 32:10-13

"As an eagle stirs up her nest

Flutters over her young,

Spreads abroad her wings, takes them,

Bears them on her wings;

So The Lord alone did lead them

And there was no strange god with them.

He made them ride on the high places of the earth"...

"He found them in a desert land,

And in a waste howling wilderness;

He led them about.

The author, Carol Bo Howell at 78 years old.

JEREMIAH 33:2 -3

Thus saith the LORD the maker thereof,
the LORD that formed it, to establish it;
the LORD is his name;
Call unto me, and I will answer thee,
and show thee great and mighty things,
which thou knowest not.

A typical church in the Philippines.

www.ingramcontent.com/pod-product-compliance
Lightning Source LLC
Chambersburg PA
CBHW070450050426
42451CB00015B/3425